ADHD
ACTIVITIES FOR
TEENS 13-18

Fun Guide to Manage your Emotions, Boost Self-esteem, Discover your Talents, and Build Confidence

By

R. Warren

The Star Publications

CONTENTS

A NOTE FOR PARENTS

Dear Parents,

Visualize yourself in the middle of a video game where everything is happening at the same time. Every sensation, sound, and sight serves as a diversion. That's roughly what it's like for people with ADHD to go through an average day.

It can be challenging for you to look after your kids if you don't know what they want or need from you. You picking up this book to learn about them and their needs better is definitely a step in the right direction.

Anyone who knows a teen with Attention Deficit Hyperactivity Disorder (ADHD) or who has ADHD themselves should read this book. This guide will assist you in understanding what ADHD is, how it can influence us, and how to thrive despite having it with the help of engaging and fun activities.

Do you believe that being forgetful, disorganized, hyperactive, or impulsive is all that ADHD is? At least I felt that before I delved into ADHD to help my daughter only to find out that I couldn't have been more wrong.

More than most people are aware that ADHD has a wide range of symptoms. But they all boil down to one thing; your child needs a different set of rules and boundaries than others. They need you to incorporate activities and chores in their daily routines to keep them engaged.

Teenagers have enough problems and drama in their life. They just need some compassion, support, and thoughtfulness from you to continue their life journey in the right direction. So, remember to support them through this book and help them navigate the challenges associated with ADHD.

A NOTE FOR TEENAGERS

Dear Reader,

Do you feel as though you are continuously being criticized for not working hard enough? That you aren't paying attention? Or that you are too impulsive? If so, you are not alone! Teenagers with ADHD frequently note that they feel misinterpreted. They are often characterized as being impulsive, hyperactive, or inattentive. But, what exactly do these terms mean?

ADHD is generally portrayed negatively, with the focus placed on the individual's limitations rather than their strengths. Should we always view ADHD for its challenges, or are there times when it might be perceived as a strength? We may better comprehend our exceptional and magnificent brains, and perceive them for what they are—different ways of viewing the world—by simply re-examining the terminology we use to define ADHD.

Which is exactly what you need to do—refine what you think and believe ADHD is and make it your superpower. It is important to realize that you can only make life easier by taking its charge. Having ADHD means you have to do things differently and you have to work a bit more to identify things that interest you the most. If you can figure that out, you can get to heights all by yourself.

This book has been specifically designed to help you on this journey with several activities to nudge you in the right direction. By practicing these activities, you can allow yourself to maintain your concentration on your tasks and enhance your level of attention, emotional capacity and more. Remember, you can take control of your life and achieve all your goals while overcoming challenges associated with ADHD.

INTRODUCTION

As with anything, managing ADHD starts with first understanding what it looks like, especially in teens, and then working through its limitations and symptoms to explore which ones you relate to the most. Once you have done that, step two is to find ways to limit or completely suppress the negative aspects and convert the positives into your strengths.

Teenagers with ADHD frequently have trouble focusing, remaining still, and controlling impulsive behavior. They may struggle to learn, connect with fellow students, and behave appropriately at home or school. In other instances, they may resist their parents' instructions for hours on homework and numerous other things like tidying their rooms or finishing their house chores.

Teens may experience low self-esteem due to these difficulties, raising their risk of showing signs of depression, anxiousness, or rebellious behavior. Functions like focus, memorization, impulsive behavior, speed of processing, and the capacity to follow instructions are frequently impaired in teens with ADHD.

However, it is essential to note that none of these challenges are impossible to fix or manage; there are several activities and suggestions in this book for you and guidance for your parents to work through each of these challenges. You will discover that employing the skills and abilities in the correct order maximizes their effectiveness and go on a fun journey to manage your emotions, increase your self-esteem, discover your abilities, and increase your confidence.

The activities in this book will describe the techniques and assist you in practicing them at home. All of the strategies in our book are based on real-life practice and success, i.e., they are tactics that have undergone analysis and are considered successful. These activities have been helpful to many teens, and we hope they will be for you as well.

CHAPTER 1 YOU HAVE ADHD SO WHAT

ADHD is not a life sentence; it is not an impairment, either. For you to believe it, you first have to act like it too. You can never live your life with ease if you are too worried about what anyone else will think.

Whenever you feel like things are not going your way and you need to clear your mind, just say this: So what if I have ADHD? So what if I feel overwhelmed? I can overcome this, even anything.

It may take some time for you to actually believe it, but it is necessary for you to start somewhere. Make it your new mantra! "So what if I have ADHD? I can do it all."

1.1 WHAT IS ADHD

A developmental illness known as ADHD is characterized by a persistent pattern of hyperactivity, impulsivity, and/or inattention. It starts in early childhood and can last into adolescence and adulthood, and can hinder routine activities and interpersonal relationships.

ADHD is a neurological condition that is associated with poor executive functioning skills. One needs executive skills to control emotions, act autonomously, realize when assistance is required, create and achieve objectives, and initiate just about anything. The frontal lobes of the brain are also engaged in ADHD, which frequently exhibits itself as delays in maturation. Therefore, teens with ADHD need more support from their families and friends to help them mature. People who have ADHD require more assistance, comprehension, and direction than those who do not and there is nothing wrong with it. A key step to managing ADHD is being open and willing to ask others for help when you need it.

There is no such thing as an average ADHD teenager. The severity of the symptoms and functional limitations varies depending on the gender, type of ADHD, environment, personal strengths, and any co-occurring issues.

In general, as children grow into teens, they show fewer of the hyperactive signs associated with ADHD. This is good news! However, as teenagers reach high school, managing ADHD effectively can become quite difficult due to the much higher expectations for them both socially and academically.

Imagine a chart where the line for expectations and demands is rising up, and the one for discipline and supervision is going down. Start of the teenage marks the point where the two lines intersect, beyond which the expectations are higher than the supervision. Teenagers are expected to be prepared to handle increasing independence as they mature, including less instances of nuisances at their homes and schools and less teaching and parental guidance, making it more challenging for them to manage ADHD in certain instances. Additionally, when children gradually distance themselves from their families and other role models during their teenage years, they become more vulnerable to influence from their peers. Some of the areas where teenagers struggle the most are described below:

Academic Performance

Teenagers with ADHD often have lower grades, and worse scores on standardized achievement tests, higher levels of school failure, and increased rates of suspension for misbehavior when they lack support. Even if the teenager doesn't have significant issues with hyperactivity or impulsivity, signs of inattention and trouble organizing themselves can be very damaging once educational demands are raised.

Interactions with Peers

Teenagers with ADHD typically struggle with peer relationships. According to research, teens with ADHD have fewer mutually beneficial friendships and are more prone to be shunned or rejected by their peers. Additionally, they are more inclined to bully others or become the target of bullying. They might not listen to friends, miss critical social cues, make rash decisions, or be intrusive due to weak social and communication skills.

Emotional Intelligence

All children experience an emotional rollercoaster during the adolescent years. Still, those with ADHD are more likely to have issues with emotion management, which could lead to more extreme highs and lows. They may find it particularly challenging to manage their frustration because of their emotional impulsivity. Both they and the people around them may find it difficult.

Substance Abuse

ADHD adolescents are more likely to experiment with tobacco, alcohol, and illegal drugs at an earlier age than their counterpart peer group. Later, they frequently have greater rates of substance abuse, smoking, and difficulties related to alcohol.

1.2 IDENTIFYING YOUR ADHD TYPE

People with ADHD exhibit recurring patterns of the following symptoms:

- **Impulsivity:** reacting before thinking or having trouble exercising self-control.

- **Inattention:** having trouble focusing.

- **Hyperactivity:** being too energetic or roaming around a lot.

Everyone has moments of impulsivity, inattention, or hyperactivity in their lives. All young people share these qualities to some extent. However, these traits are more pronounced in youngster with ADHD, but it's important to keep in mind that we should not view these three traits solely through a negative lens; each one presents its own unique set of difficulties and opportunities.

The Three Main Characteristics of ADHD	Challenges	Advantages
Inattention	Having trouble concentrating on things. Being Forgetful - inability to focus, daydreaming, and being easily bored. Inability to follow a logical progression of actions or thoughts. Getting distracted with ease. Inability to start a task or make a decision - A sign of procrastination. Impaired memory both short term and long term.	Artistic. Appreciates the thrill of unusual situations and activities. A strong capacity for 'visual imagery,' or the ability to visualize in images. Creative thinking - The ability to think creatively and independently.
Impulsivity	Not considering the repercussions of one's actions before acting on them. Unorganized. Interrupting other people's thoughts and conversations.	Inquisitive. Highly motivated. Imaginative. Thinkers with original ideas. Concentrated on finding solutions.
Hyper-activeness	Fiddling and fumbling. Trouble remaining still for long periods of time. Being in need of constant motion.	Full of energy. Motivated. Devoted to work. Enthusiastic.

Some individuals with ADHD primarily exhibit signs of inattention. Others display signs of impulsivity and hyperactivity. Both forms of symptoms can occur in certain other individuals. Inattentive behavior may manifest as:

- Trouble maintaining focus during play and tasks, including talks, tests, or extended assignments.

- Failure to pay close attention when talked to directly.

- Not paying attention to every detail or committing seemingly reckless errors in studies or during other activities.

- Having trouble organizing activities and tasks, such as carrying out tasks in a specific order and keeping materials and personal possessions in order.

- Trouble trying to manage time and working under pressure.

- Avoiding activities that require continued mental activity, such as homework.

- Losing things essential for activities and tasks, including classroom supplies, books, and accessories.

- Having trouble following through on guidelines or finishing chores.

Symptoms of impulsivity and hyperactivity may include:

- Inability to play or participate in hobbies quietly.

- Constant movement or acting as if powered by a motor.

- Wiggling and squirming while seated.

- Getting up and roaming around when instructed to remain seated, such as in a classroom.

- Trying to run, leaping around, or trying to climb at inappropriate moments.

- Talking too much.

- Finishing other people's sentences or responding to questions before they have been properly asked.

- Having trouble waiting for one's turn, such as when in line.

- Interrupting or interfering with others when they are engaged in activities, games, or conversations.

1.3 HOW CAN YOU CONTROL THE IMPULSIVE URGES

Before you know how to control impulsive urges, it is essential to learn how impulsivity can manifest itself in teens with ADHD. In general, impulsive behavior frequently appears as an unplanned, impromptu course of action that is not supported by reasoning. Your emotions influence your behavior. These spontaneous acts may occasionally conflict with your own objectives and routines, and on rare occasions, they may endanger you or others. Impulsive actions include:

- Frequently interrupting others or saying things you eventually regret.

- Jumping from one task to the next or attempting to manage several tasks at the same time.

- Coming back with more items than you thought you will buy at the supermarket.

Important Skills to Master

Planning and Prioritizing
Taking the time to think about the information you need, in which order, to create a plan to complete a piece of work.

Self-Monitoring
Knowing where you are up to with a task and what to do next.

Impulse Control
How to control and regulate how you feel so you can motivate yourself or get yourself into a learning state of mind or the right "frame of mind" to do a particular task or manage a particular situation.

Working Memory
Remembering lots of information in the forefront of your mind to complete a task or for problem solving.

Task Initiation
Getting yourself ready to start a task and finding which actions you need to take in order to start a task.

Flexible Thinking
Changing how you think or working to meet the demands of the task.

Goal Setting
Understanding out motivation what we want to achieve and making a plan to ensure that we achieve our goals.

Emotional Control
Managing our feelings to complete the task in hand.

The majority of people occasionally act impulsively, but the hyperactive-impulsive subtype of ADHD, in particular, has an impact on impulse control to the point where these behaviors persist over time in varying contexts. The following methods for impulse control may be helpful.

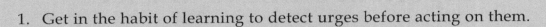
1. Get in the habit of learning to detect urges before acting on them.

2. Give that urge a name. For instance, "I feel angry right now."

3. Figure out which action your emotion wants you to take. For instance, "I'm angry, and I want to blame my friend."

4. Decide what you must do to put an end to your impulsive behavior. For instance, "I need to communicate my annoyance without taking it personally." Or you may say, "I need to leave, take a break, and return later."

5. Reassess the situation after your need has subsided.

6. Write down your emotions, what you wanted to do, and what you actually did.

7. Divide your tasks into manageable portions. For instance, spend 30 minutes on your task and then have a five-minute break somewhere else.

8. When you're taking a break, schedule quick, soothing activities. Additionally, set an alarm. If you take too long of a break, you can become distracted or start working on other things.

9. Continue to inquire about the task you're finding challenging. For instance, "How horrible can this truly be?" or "Can I motivate myself through the challenging parts?" or "How great will it feel when I'm done?"

Take Part in Relaxing Activities

Perlman claims that stress or being on edge might occasionally cause impulsivity in people with ADHD. Your ability to resist impulses can improve by relaxing. Perlman offers the following advice:

- Experiment with guided imagery.

- Always listen to soothing music, especially when trying to be productive.

- Use deep breathing exercises throughout the day.

- Work out as frequently as you can.

- Acquire the skill of progressive muscular relaxation.

Adolescent Instabilities Correlate with ADHD

During adolescence, the human brain undergoes significant changes. Everyone finds this difficult, but teens with ADHD especially so because of their unique neurodevelopmental characteristics. Teens and ADHD intersect to provide a human experience that is frequently fraught with difficulties. I've heard from many people with ADHD who say that the teenage was the most challenging time in their lives.

Some regions of the brain evolve earlier than others during the long, multi-year process of adolescent brain development. The prefrontal cortex, which is engaged in developing self-control and making all decisions, does not fully grow until the mid-20s. In contrast, the limbic system, engaged in emotional response and reward-seeking behavior, gains maturity early in adolescence.

Teenagers may be more susceptible to the limbic system's preference for instant gratification due to this deficit in brain maturity if the prefrontal cortex's capacity for long-term and structural thinking does not provide sufficiently robust checks and balances. These same neurological circuits are also impacted by ADHD, which in a way, intensifies the difficulties associated with adolescence.

Teenagers with ADHD particularly struggle to learn from experience due to this. What we pay close attention to, whatever we decide to do, how effectively we learn and remember, and how we resist impulses to behave wrongly are all controlled by reward impulses in our brains. ADHD impacts all these processes, and teens with ADHD may require more severe or immediate consequences to push them to do suitable activities sufficiently.

1.4 ROLE OF PARENTS AND FAMILY IN AN ADHD DIAGNOSIS

All teenagers need support and understanding from their families and friends. Parents can show this support by hearing their teens out and offering solutions that could benefit them. However, it is imperative for teens with ADHD to recognize their needs, and that they can identify their problems and solutions themselves. At the same time, teens need to understand that they may require input from others to overcome challenges. This is where family and friends come in. They can support this by maintaining records with the teenagers and creating schedules they should follow to make a balanced routine.

Parents and siblings, along with friends, can offer insights into their working order and how you can improve different aspects of your lives for the better.

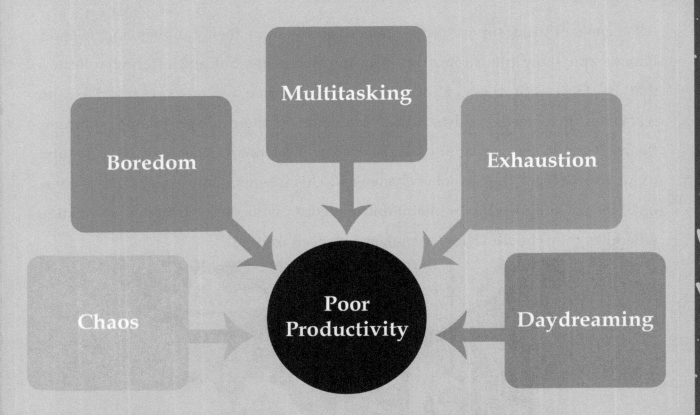

Lessen the Clutter. Teens with ADHD must be more organized and less distracted in order to be productive.

Disorder, or the chance for uncontrolled randomness in a teen's day creates an ideal setting for inadequate concentration and focus. A teenager may attempt to complete their work or complete chores only to become sidetracked by a myriad of other interactions and activities. As a result, the work is only partially completed, and the parents feel distraught. Setting up a schedule will keep you on track. You can find ways to prevent external chaotic distractions from interfering with your workflow in addition to creating a routine, such as:

- Turning off any media interruptions, such as the TV, until work is complete.

- Finding a quiet space to complete your homework (preferably somewhere other than your own bedroom)

- Listening to music while trying to complete a task to block out outside noise.

- Using lists that can provide step-by-step directions for tasks.

Eliminate Boredom. For teens with ADHD to be productive, they require stimulation and engagement.

Teens with ADHD tend to get bored easily and might not feel driven to continue an activity if it is not thrilling or exciting to them. Unfortunately, doing chores and homework is rarely enjoyable. Here are three elements you may add to assist if you frequently find that your to-do list is dull or uninspiring:

1. Increase Difficulty or Competitiveness - Many teens with ADHD become more involved in a project when the difficulty level is raised. Simply apply a timer or compete against a sibling in sibling clean-off when the work seems dull or pointless. At the conclusion of the task, include an incentive to increase motivation.

2. Add Music - Play your favorite music as you work, but with caution (you don't want to create distractions, of course). The distraction-seeking behaviors frequently associated with ADHD may be reduced with this additional stimulation.

3. Include Food - Having a snack while doing your homework can enhance the amount of engagement just enough to aid concentration, similar to how music can.

Cut back on Multitasking. Teens with ADHD believe themselves to be expert multitaskers... They are certainly not.

ADHD-afflicted youngsters are significantly more easily distracted than typical teenagers. Distractibility frequently results in overstimulation and performing too many things concurrently. Inefficiency results from this, which causes the task to seem much more challenging to do.

According to research, multitasking is a type of fragmented attention, which might reduce productivity. Teens with ADHD could pretend to be multitasking when they are being distracted. Here are some ideas to try if you have a tendency to start your task but then switching to other activities before finishing it:

Put away the cell phone: On the subject of multitasking, your phone is most likely to be blamed. You may have countless other pleasurable activities at your disposal; therefore, it is understandable why you might lack the motivation to complete your chores.

You can also try reducing the number of commitments or to-dos delivered at once if the phone isn't the issue. Try assigning yourself one task at a time using clear instructions rather than picking up a long list of tasks.

Decrease Fantasizing: Teens with ADHD frequently use daydreaming to cope

against frustration. Teens with ADHD generally expect a challenging experience when they sit down to complete tasks. They recognize that it will require a considerable amount of time and concentration to maintain focus and get through their task, not because they need to be more intelligent.

Many young people find themselves daydreaming about less difficult things to do and hoping that they will do something different and more fun. They may be sitting there contemplating how much they would like to play Xbox as they stare blankly at their textbook. This type of internal diversion prevents people from finishing the task in question since it causes them to dissociate from the present. So, instead of diverting your attention, focus on how you can quickly complete your work so you may be able to do other tasks that interest you more after.

Set a Timer: During a study session, set a reminder to sound once every five or ten minutes. This will remind you to get back to your task. Productivity is significantly less negatively impacted by three minutes of a diversion than by thirty.

Make Work Relevant: Tell yourself that once you complete your assignments, chores, or other duties, you can access the more fun activity you want to be doing, such as playing Xbox or watching YouTube. By doing this, you will be aware that these pursuits are within your grasp and are only on the opposite side of the challenging work rather than daydreaming about them. Remind yourself if you start to get sidetracked, "Once I finish my homework, I can play Xbox."

By encouraging yourself to be more attentive, you can deal with these situations in a more effective manner.

Prevent Fatigue. Teenagers with ADHD put a lot of effort into concentrating and remaining still.

Teens with ADHD struggle to maintain their focus at school and work, so when they get home, they don't have much energy left over to complete other pressing duties. The fact that ADHD drugs sometimes start to wear away later in the day makes this situation worse.

The teenage brain, fortunately, is undergoing fast growth and development. This implies that you will get more resilient and stronger as you learn to push past fatigue and a lack of enthusiasm. Of course, exerting that kind of pressure is not easy. You might attempt the following strategies to assist yourself in overcoming the tiredness slump:

- **Recognize and Reward Efforts** - Let yourself know when you go above and beyond or persevere through challenging tasks even when they are weary! Applaud your work ethic and encourage yourself.

- **Make Space for Resting** - Ensure you have enough time to rest. You can feel exhausted by the obligations of school, athletics, friends, and family time even before the workday is through. Make an effort to plan aside time to allow yourself to express your feelings and recharge.

- **Establish Reasonable Expectations** - Parents want their kids to achieve and reach their full potential. Occasionally, without taking into account their individual goals or being reasonable, they can pressurize their teenagers to work harder. To avoid this, spend some time with your parents to establish reasonable standards of achievement and how they can assist you in your development.

CHAPTER 2 MANAGING EMOTIONAL DEVELOPMENT

For many teens with ADHD, emotional management is a difficult issue. Strong emotions overwhelm teens' still-evolving coping mechanisms, whether they take the form of extreme grief, excessive anxiety, or irrational outbursts of anger. They cannot make difficult decisions, think clearly, or weigh the implications of their actions while under pressure. Their developing capacity for executive functioning means they have a hard time controlling their reactions and learning to relax. The situation calls for assistance.

First and foremost, learn to self-regulate. Your irritation fuels your anger.

Everybody has had those moments when they wish they could take back something they said out of exasperation. As adults, we have the power to regain control and place those feelings in their proper context thanks to our developed thinking brain. However, teens with ADHD require additional support to master this competency since their prefrontal lobes do not complete growing until the age of 25 or later. Keeping this viewpoint in mind, you need to be willing to receive help from others around you to regulate your emotions, preserve your patience, and keep your cool when you're on the edge of losing it.

Obviously, controlling your emotions doesn't imply you'll never feel angry; you are a human and will experience emotions. The distinction is that you are able to recognize when you are getting agitated and work on calming yourself down. You put an end to what you're doing, take a few deep breaths, halt the action, and refocus.

Reduce the likelihood of your triggers for emotional outbursts. Encourage yourself to plan your day, avoid multitasking, eat properly, get enough sleep, engage in stress-relieving activities, and participate in an exercise regimen. Plan some time to unwind and concentrate, especially if you also struggle with sensory issues.

Managing ADHD is about capitalizing on your inherent skills and competencies.

Teenagers must understand that they can improve their daily life, routine, and overall quality of living if they play to their own unique strengths. They may be a little different from others regarding their needs, but they can compete with them through their naturally gifted abilities. The only difference is that they must look for their passions and interests to succeed.

2.1 UNDERSTANDING YOUR EMOTIONS

Controlling emotions also referred to as "emotional regulation," is a task that many teens with ADHD find challenging. It's challenging for teens to learn to comprehend and regulate their emotions. Emotional control may be much more challenging for people with ADHD. *Why do you suppose that is?* Teens with ADHD may find it more difficult for a variety of reasons.

- Various brain regions mature at varying rates, and many different brain regions must cooperate or synchronize for our executive functioning talents to function.

- Another factor is the realization that we can't always do what we want to as teenagers. As our brains grow, we get better equipped to plan ahead and draw lessons from our past achievements and failures to make better decisions in future.

- We also learn when to speak and do nothing as we start to recognize the sentiments, perspectives, and ideas of others, even if we disagree with them.

- As teenagers, friendships become a more terrific source of motivation. Friends take on a significant role in our lives. We all yearn to fit in with a group of friends, to be liked and valued. We start to recognize our values in life and realize that these values serve as our motivation. In actuality, our motivation increases as we get older because of the individuals we respect.

To build and develop strong friendships with friends yet still accomplish our own individual and educational goals, teenagers with ADHD must learn how to manage their emotions.

2.2 UTILIZING THE HYPERFOCUS

The term ADHD may convey that a person with this condition cannot concentrate or pay close attention to anything. This is incorrect, though, as ADHD is a problem with attention regulation rather than the absence of it.

Teens with ADHD struggle hard to concentrate on dull, routine tasks, but they concentrate very well on things that interest them. In fact, their level of concentration is exceptionally high, known as hyperfocus, when working on a fascinating task.

Parents, teachers, and friends may be frustrated by an individual's propensity to hyperfocus, resulting in remarks like, "They can concentrate when they choose to." However, focusing requires more than simply a desire to do so. Many people with ADHD desire to concentrate, whether on a lesson or what their friend is saying, but they can only focus intensely on something when it is the ideal combination of personally engaging, stimulating, and rewarding.

The Indications of Hyperfocus

When someone is hyper-focused, they get so absorbed in what they are doing that they lose track of everything else around them. They have a type of tunnel vision that enables them to focus all of their attention and effort on the current task.

For instance, they could become so preoccupied with finishing a task or completing a project that they may neglect to eat a meal or even get to bed, and they may lose themselves for hours in a video game while playing.

This behavior needs to be addressed if you are struggling with maintaining order in your daily routine due to your hyperfocus.

What Causes Hyperfocus?

Hyperfocus, like distractibility, is thought to be caused by an incredibly low level of dopamine that is especially active in the brain's frontal lobes. Due to this dopamine shortage, it is challenging to "change gears" and engage in monotonous but required work.

Is Hyperfocus Associated with ADHD a Negative Trait?

Hyperfocus doesn't necessarily have any adverse effects. In fact, it might be advantageous. It is possible, for instance, for some people with ADHD to direct their energy into a worthwhile pursuit, like a project at work or school. Some people reward themselves after finishing tedious but crucial work by allowing themselves to be hyper-focused on something else. It helps them cope with the boredom of monotony they feel.

Advantages of Hyperfocus

There are several benefits of being hyperfocus, both for teens with and without ADHD. For example, you can ignore everything else and concentrate solely on meeting a deadline when there is one. You establish an image as an individual who is competent and devoted to their work if you are hyper-focused on work-related tasks. Additionally, it implies that you take pleasure in your profession. You could show close attention and attractiveness to the individual you are dating in the early stages of a relationship, making you more appealing and attractive.

An activity that boosts a teen's self-esteem could capture their intense attention. This is excellent news because having ADHD can damage a person's self-esteem. The feeling you get from taking action is more significant than the activity itself, whether you are trying to learn to skateboard or any software.

An individual's capacity to remain "*in the zone,*" focused, and absorbed in a task for hours may result in some important innovations and creations.

2.3 ACTIVITIES

Teens can never learn emotional interaction through words of advice or other people's meddling. The following activities can help you in building emotional connections with others that are deep and meaningful. Try them to reinforce behavior in yourself that you need to practice without the stress of making a fool of yourself in front of others.

INTERACTING WITH PETS

Teenagers who suffer from ADHD might benefit from simply having a pet in the family. Here are some of the reasons why:

- Taking care of a pet can help develop time management skills. It requires a lot of planning to feed and care for them.

- Taking a dog on a walk and engaging in playful interaction with them is an excellent way to release pent-up energy.

- Pets provide unconditional affection and companionship.

- Petting and caressing an animal might help you feel less anxious and stressed.

- Socializing can be facilitated by having a pet. Animals draw attention and make excellent conversation starters.

- Teenagers can learn empathy by taking care of an animal. Some teens with ADHD have difficulties in this area.

Pets are an excellent choice for anyone that needs to work on their emotional intelligence and interactions. Pets can be pretty persuasive creatures in letting you open up without the fear of becoming an outcast. They offer a chance to forge long-lasting bonds with no judgment or expectations, which is what most teens suffering from ADHD need to work on.

WRITING & JOURNALING

Writing is used in this activity to investigate one's thoughts and feelings. It would be best if you made it a point to develop a writing routine in which you can jot down your thoughts and then think over what you've written. It allows you to process your feelings in a protected environment and in a manner unique to you. People might, for instance, write about their life in a journal or create creative works such as poetry or stories made up entirely of their own imagination. Journal writing will allow you to record your thoughts and responses, which you can later use to interact with others.

SOLVING JIGSAW PUZZLES AND MAZES

These are excellent tools for teens with ADHD, despite their simplicity.

You may find age-appropriate mazes for teenagers online for free. Start with the simple ones and work your way up. Observe your pace and mistakes. Mazes are excellent for increasing processing speed, planning, focus, and visual-motor coordination.

Puzzle games and all of these activities assist in the development of the brain, making them excellent for teenagers with ADHD and other learning impairments. There are maze games where players control a tiny marble over difficult obstacles inside a transparent sphere. You can modify the challenges to make different games.

In the same way, crossword puzzles enhance word recognition and sequencing skills. Similarly, pictorial puzzles that require searching for objects that are difficult to find or finding things that are "wrong" in the picture will help you to focus and pay attention.

LISTENING TO RELAXING MUSIC

When used therapeutically, music may profoundly affect a person's disposition and level of anxiety. All aspects of human health, including emotions, memories, and relationships, can benefit from music listening. Music helps areas of the brain that are underdeveloped in teenagers with ADHD and it strengthens the hearing, visual/spatial, and motor cortexes of the brain. All of these domains have connections to one another, including speech and language skills, reading comprehension, arithmetic, problem-solving, cognitive organization, concentration, and attention problems. As a result, music listening has emerged as a critical tool for assisting youth with ADHD in developing the skills required to enhance their educational outcomes and general functioning.

STORYTELLING

This activity is frequently neglected due to the fact that it appears to be uncomplicated. Nevertheless, there are substantial benefits of this activity. Engaging in this activity can bring about positive changes in people's life since it offers the chance for individuals to grow and develop on a personal level. However, there is more to the narrative than just reading. It is an essential means of expression, self-reflection, and gaining an awareness of the world around us. When trying to make someone else understand a story, it is necessary to have comprehension, attention, and proper delivery.

Storytelling is a form of art that can assist in the development of a more profound comprehension and connections to our community, culture, and history by using narratives to retell events. Thinking about the story's many distinct characters is another helpful activity for teens with ADHD. Teens with ADHD can improve their skills in analyzing characters, digesting complex ideas and concepts, and sharpening their concentration on the intricacies of a story by getting involved in the narrative.

Teens who have ADHD can have a more detailed awareness of a variety of perspectives and experiences when they listen to and tell stories. It enables individuals to cultivate compassion, become far more conscious of the myriad perspectives that exist around the world, and discover innovative approaches to critical thinking.

DRAWING, PAINTING AND ART RELATED ACTIVITIES

Teen's patience and cognitive abilities can be put to the test through art-related activities. The openness and inventiveness that art encourages makes it one of the finest activities for brain stimulation. Art also helps in expressing feelings and discovering individuality. Teens can get better at critical thinking and solving problems, improve their mental health, and feel better about themselves by doing art.

In this activity, people use visual arts to process their feelings, ideas, or experiences, such as painting, sculpture and sketching.

Through art making, teenagers can develop a stronger sense of purpose and self-expression, which enables them to deal with challenging feelings or situations and creates a greater awareness of the world around them. Art also assists teenagers in developing a knowledge of their individuality.

LEARNING MUSICAL INSTRUMENTS

Music takes a higher level of attention to detail than other pursuits. It requires practice and notes memorization. A teenager with ADHD will be able to learn rhythms and how to follow along with a song by singing. Teens with ADHD can improve their concentration and organizational abilities by participating in this activity. Playing an instrument may also be a lot of fun, keeping you engaged.

An ADHD teen's emotional response to music can have a profoundly positive effect. Teenagers may not have had the chance to concentrate and express themselves creatively, but music may serve as a form of meditation. Many adolescents with ADHD find relief from their symptoms when they take up an instrument, which allows them to channel their pent-up emotions in a constructive and personally meaningful way.

VISITING INTERACTIVE PLACES

Emotional attachment is not only with things and pets. It can be with places too. It could be an old park you visited in childhood or a museum you love to explore. Anything that holds your interest is recommended. It can be anywhere as long as it excites you and stimulates your interest. *You might be wondering why?* Simply because managing ADHD is all about making sure your interests are given the same level of priority that they deserve. It will allow you to change your interests and expectations into experiences you can learn from.

CHAPTER 3 WORKING ON SOCIAL DEVELOPMENT

We engage and communicate with others around us on a daily basis using social skills. We do this through verbal and nonverbal means of communication (i.e., by making and maintaining eye contact, smiling and nodding, and using other physical cues as well as verbal cues like volume, tone of voice, speed, etc.). Understanding and using these social skills might be challenging for teens with ADHD.

The executive functioning deficit in their brains may make it difficult for them to develop and maintain acquaintances. Executive control in the brain controls a person's capacity to wait for their turn, refrain from becoming sidetracked, direct their activities, restrain their feelings, and use working memory to react in social situations. Teens with ADHD may demonstrate a delay in executive function in comparison to their peers.

Social Challenges Have a Cyclical Structure

Teenagers with ADHD may struggle to understand and respond to the norms and expectations of a group environment, including learning to share, take turns, listen, and understand facial expressions. They frequently show signs of boredom, distraction, or disinterest and tune out the speaker. Teens with ADHD can struggle to control their emotions during peer interactions and are susceptible to feeling overburdened, irritable, or frustrated.

When teenagers with ADHD become preoccupied or take over social situations, their classmates may see them as indifferent and rude. Peers will likely steer clear of these teens, resulting in lost chances to develop social skills and diminished

self-assurance. Without social connections, teens would develop feelings of inferiority and unpleasant emotional responses to social encounters. In an effort to prevent further rejection, some ADHD teenagers may even completely shun social situations.

Why is it Vital to Have Peer Relationships?

For a person to perform at their best, they need to have adequate social skills and positive peer interactions. Children learn to collaborate, bargain, and solve problems with others when they have positive connections with their peers. These skills enable them to establish fruitful interactions with their peers. Social supports are, therefore, protective elements. They provide people with a feeling of acceptance, compassion, and belonging. As kids approach puberty, they get more dependent on peer connection and are more sensitive to social cues. Through regular social encounters, friendships educate teenagers on how to get along with others, solve issues, see things from other people's perspectives, handle peer disagreements, and accept people from different backgrounds.

3.1 INTERACTING WITH OTHERS

Teens who have ADHD frequently display behavior that is impulsive, disorganized, aggressive, excessively sensitive, passionate, emotional, or disruptive. They frequently misinterpret and miscommunicate with people in their social surroundings, including their parents, siblings, classmates, friends, and teachers.

The capacity of teens with ADHD to control their behavior and responses to others is impaired. Relationships may become extremely strained and fragile as a result of this.

Due to their inattention, impulsivity, and hyperactivity, teens with ADHD frequently struggle in social situations, feel rejected by others, and have communication difficulties. Such unfavorable interpersonal consequences induce emotional anguish and suffering. They appear to have a role in the development of co-occurring depression and anxiety disorders as well.

One must be responsible, pay attention, and have self-control over impulsive actions to communicate with people effectively. Teens with ADHD are frequently forgetful and inattentive and frequently exhibit poor impulse control. If you want to communicate effectively, just start by talking to others. You might like them, or you may not. The important thing is to try. It is all about finding the people best for you.

Having ADHD is not a life's bane. You can create a meaningful relationship with someone if they are on the same pitch as you are; before you find that kind of person, practice with others. Who knows, you might find others not too bad either. Some may need you to explain your behavior, but you can definitely find people who are

great for you and your mental health.

Educating people on ADHD may reduce much of the tension and blame circulating about ADHD and the dynamics of its impacts on interpersonal interactions and behaviors. The person with ADHD must also study techniques to improve as much as practicable in social skills. You can try activities given in section 3.4 of this book to help you improve your social skills.

3.2 FINDING COMMON GROUNDS

Teenagers with ADHD sometimes have little awareness of how their classmates see them and will make social mistakes without even realizing them. However, it is important to note that teenagers are in a stage in their lives where they can work on themselves by learning the norms. Teenage friendships are frequently closer and more personal than those between younger children and can be used to anticipate greater understanding and compassion from their pals.

To overcome the challenges of social interactions for teens with ADHD, teens must learn how to find common ground with the people they interact with. Teens must be able to communicate and listen, share, think before they act, respect boundaries, recognize other people's social cues, take turns, learn to hear other people's viewpoints, and be receptive to other people's ideas, feelings, and welfare in order to enjoy these types of connections.

Finding the common ground is all about looking out for the people that share your interest and passions. The main building block of any relationship is shared interest. If you have something to talk about, there is a great chance you can build on that foundation to grow a friendship. It can make it easier for you to maintain such friendships by forging a life-like bond.

Teenagers with ADHD may need assistance in learning how to manage the complex emotions and social circumstances that come with making new acquaintances. By

engaging in activities and games that can bridge their gaps from others, they can easily fit in social circles they deem fit for themselves.

3.3 BOOSTING YOUR SELF-ESTEEM

A social process contributes significantly to the formation of an individual's sense of self-esteem. One of the primary reasons individuals get the experience of being valuable and special is because they are seen as important and exceptional by the friends and social groups to which they belong.

Teens who believe they play a significant part in their family, peer groups, community, and culture are more likely to feel better about themselves. Due to this, teens should ensure that they seek chances from their parents to join recreational institutions and have ample time necessary to engage with others. The chance to participate in social events and festivities also benefits teens. They must get familiar with their background and have a sense of ownership over it.

Teenagers can engage with many different individuals as they join various groups at school and in the community, some similar to themselves and some significantly different. They just need to get out of their comfort zones and try talking to others. The diversity of people groups and ages can offer them chances to develop and sustain various relations with friends and adults in several roles.

Develop Your Social Skills

Teenagers with ADHD, for instance, may appear withdrawn or silent when they are having trouble paying attention. Teenagers who have trouble focusing and remembering could also forget to reply to DMs, giving the impression that they don't care about their friends. However, that is not true!

One of the biggest causes of poor self-esteem in teens with ADHD is rejection by peers. Even if you cannot control how you interact with others, try practicing your

social skills. The only way to improve is to open yourself to learning and relearning. It may take time, but only practice will make your skills near perfect.

3.4 ACTIVITIES

Most teens require assistance at one point or the other to learn social skills. These abilities can require additional practice for teens with ADHD. This is because they may struggle to focus, restrain impulsive behavior, and manage hyperactivity.

The activities given below can help in the learning process of social skills for teens who struggle with socialization among their peer group. These activities will help you immerse yourself in them but also engage other people with you. By performing these activities, you will be able to interact with others properly in ways that are not forced but enjoyable for all.

CHARADES

All you need for charades is a bag filled with slips of paper with scribblings on them. You might use popular movies, TV shows, or books. You then "play out" whats on the slip e.g. by creating a cube with your fingers for a TV, opening a book for a book, or rolling the camera for a movie.

The papers should include clues on them that a reader can play out without speaking, keeping the audience guessing. If there is a large gathering, divide yourselves into teams and compete against each other. Let one team member act while the opposing team guesses, and then swap places.

BOARD GAME

Board games have existed forever, and they continue to improve. Teens with short attention spans will benefit from them because they must learn to wait for their turn and concentrate on their next move. Through board games, teens are better able to concentrate on cognitive processing, strategic thinking, and problem-solving as a result.

Unlike video games, board games encourage conversation and social interaction. Therefore, board games are a fantastic tool to for teens to learn valuable skills that they may apply in their daily life.

DIY LASER MAZE

You can create a maze for yourself to climb through by taping crepe paper strips in different settings along the wall from one side to the other. The objective is to cross the paper without touching or damaging any of it as you go! For this activity, you will need strips of paper or crepe paper, sellotape, or masking tape.

PASTA RELAY RACE

You can either do this activity inside or outside using raw pasta. Start by splitting the players into two teams. Place two sizable, empty pots in one corner or side, and instruct the teams to fall in line behind them. Have two sizable pots of dried pasta on the opposite side or corner. Give a ladle or a sizable wooden spoon to each squad.

Next, each team member runs to the pasta pot, fills the ladle, and then sprints over to the emptied pot to dump the pasta before sprinting back to the team. The winner of the race is the team that moves all of its pasta first. This game gets nasty, so beware!

Variations: Use cooked pasta, which is slick and harder to retain in the ladle, to make the game harder. You can also use spaghetti in the relay race, which can also create this activity a bit more challenging.

SQUARES

To play, you must arrange dots into a square array on a piece of paper. Then, each player takes turns to trace a line between two nearby dots. Lines can only be vertical or horizontal; they cannot be diagonal. Once you successfully complete all four side of a box, put the first letter of your name inside the box. Make as many boxes as possible while preventing the other player from making them is the goal. The contestant with the most initialed boxes wins.

PICTIONARY

Pictionary is among the most commonly played pen-and-paper games. In Pictionary, each player takes turns to draw a specific object while the other players must attempt to guess what it is. To get started, everyone must settle on a theme. For instance, participants could select to draw movies, idiomatic expressions, or particular types of phrases.

The first participant must discreetly come up with something to sketch after choosing a topic. When the drawing is finished, they can display it to the other participants, who will then have to determine what the drawing symbolizes. The next player will be able to draw something once someone correctly identifies the first player's image. You can play pictionary for pure entertainment or make it a contest by giving points for accurate guesses.

PUZZLE PIECE HUNT

Place the puzzle pieces in a different location in a room. Prepare a clear surface so that you can put the puzzle together on it. Players look for puzzle pieces, gather them on the table, and try to put the puzzle back together. If you want to play the game in groups, have each participant write their team's initials or name on the backside of the jigsaw pieces. Those with the most pieces win. You will want either an age-appropriate jigsaw puzzle or the ability to cut a huge picture into a number of smaller pieces to play this game.

CHAPTER 4 DISCOVERING YOURSELF AND BUILDING CONFIDENCE

Discovering your own self is an essential task in everyone's life. You cannot even imagine succeeding when all you can do is fear everything and everyone around you.

Building confidence does not happen in a matter of hours or days. It takes time to truly appreciate yourself and command the same respect from others. You can do the same by believing in yourself and being aware of your strengths and weaknesses.

4.1 BELIEVING IN YOURSELF

Being special and unique is never in question. Each person is the best version of themselves. It is the truth. When you believe in this philosophy, believing in yourself will also become more uncomplicated.

It can be daunting for teens to be vulnerable with others as they fear rejection. Most teens do not realize that they need to trust themselves first and believing in themselves is an essential part of their lives too. Their ability to go ahead only depends on their confidence and trust in themselves.

4.2 TRUSTING IN YOUR OWN SUPERPOWERS

Now that you know that trusting in your own self is vital for gaining confidence, it is also necessary for you to find your own superpowers. You may ask now, which superpowers? Do I even possess any? Yes, you do!

Take a minute and think about what you do best or what interests you the most. It could be anything that you love and enjoy. For example, if you love to paint, then that is your superpower. It has the potential to make you the best version of yourself. It gives you a purpose and an interest that so many others share with you. You can make it a basis of trusting in your talent and connecting with others.

4.3 RECOGNIZING YOUR UNIQUENESS FROM OTHERS

As mentioned earlier, everyone is unique and has something special to offer. It is upon you to realize it as soon as you can. Teens with ADHD have a distinct perspective that others can find valuable and intriguing.

Many people with ADHD are incredibly imaginative, creative, and original. They are the epitome of "*outside the box*" thinkers and frequently have many ideas flying around in their heads. They frequently approach things and situations from a distinct or alternate perspective. They prosper better in settings that respect their unique talents and skills, but they need to realize it themselves so they can use it to their advantage.

4.4 ACTIVITIES

Teenagers with ADHD can use these activities to learn new ways to spend their energy. You can do all these activities to gain more confidence in yourselves and your abilities. All the activities mentioned here are beneficial for teenagers and allow them to do something with their time. Who knows which activity turns out to be your own superpower!

VOLUNTEERING

You can only become good at social interactions when you start mingling with others. Volunteering in any place can help you get to know others and talk to them in a no-pressure zone.

This activity will allow you to get out of your comfort zone and practice through proper communication opportunities. It will provide you with a different setting and people you are not likely to interact with otherwise.

MARTIAL ARTS

The focus and self-control that martial arts require set it apart from other sports and hobbies. It is a challenging physical activity that supports the development of the brain's neural networks. The ability to coordinate the mind and body will help the individuals control their impulsivity.

It is also a great activity to ensure that you learn something useful and build your confidence. Martial arts is a type of activity that can be harnessed to feel good about yourself and your ability to learn new skills.

SUMMER CAMP

Not many people like summer camps. They might prefer to stay at home and relax during the holidays, but these camps are necessary for growth, especially for teens with ADHD. Such teens require all those activities that can potentially interest and engage them. Summer camps create an environment that is usually very beneficial for teens with ADHD. It allows them to work on their social skills while learning about other things that are not part of their curriculum.

They enjoy such activities because these involve less pressure from their surroundings, and they can enjoy things at their own pace. It also builds their confidence to be more actively involved in their surroundings while looking for more ways to express themselves.

WAX OR CANDLE PAINTING

For this activity, draw a picture with a candle on colored or white paper. You are going to need to exert a little bit of pressure. Then use water-based paints to cover the paper. It will reveal the candle drawing. Create something original or write covert messages. It is an excellent activity for teens who love to explore artistic outlooks and create something fun.

Good artistic value and skills can grow your confidence, which is why it is necessary to partake in such activities. It can help you to discover your own talents and create something out of nothing.

SCOUTING

What types of activities do teens with ADHD prefer? Something both entertaining and educational!

Scouting is engaging and methodical and may help teens to identify and improve their skills. Additionally, scouting may give ADHD-affected teenagers a chance to form friendships and bonds, educate them on how to take on roles and responsibilities, and boost their self-confidence.

It is also a fantastic chance for teenagers to practice taking the initiative, problem-solving abilities, and task management. Scouting can provide a teenager the chance to develop qualities and abilities they might have missed out on because of their ADHD.

WORD LADDERS

Word Ladders is an entertaining word game that has the potential to increase vocabulary. Both individuals and groups can participate in the game of word ladders. Each player in Ladder of Words requires one pen and a sheet of paper. It is typically ideal to start with three-letter words like a *cat* because participants must begin with the exact same word and write it at the top of their paper.

Fat
Rat
Rate
Date
Dates

Each player takes turns writing a new word below the one they just wrote, either with one letter added or changed from the original word. *Here is a case where the word fat is the first word. Fat, Rat, Rate, Date, Dates.* Each participant may continue until they run out of word changes. The goal is to create the longest word you can, and the player who succeeds receives a point.

This activity has the potential to not only make you learn but help you involve your peers in fun. It can help you socialize with your peers as well as keep everyone engaged with full enthusiasm. Such games are great icebreakers and a fun way to test your own knowledge.

DANCING

Dancing is an excellent activity for people with mental health issues such as stress, anxiety, and depression. They can all be helped through the use of physical movement and dance. Dancing allows for an outlet for self-expression and the processing of repressed feelings. It has also been shown to help assist in alleviating symptoms associated with mental health conditions.

There is also a selection of options available to choose from in terms of video game dancing, on the basis of a person's age and the things they enjoy doing. These games are compatible with various video game consoles, such as the Xbox, Wii, and others. In addition to that, you will need to get a dancing mat that is compatible with your system.

The teenagers can use dancing as a fun and creative approach to explore their emotions and become more conscious of feelings that might have been difficult to convey in words through these dancing activities. Dance therapy is a form of expressive therapeutic intervention.

The skills of attention, speed of processing, making preparations, synchronization, and sensory integration are all improved through playing these games. They come with the additional benefit of being a fantastic kind of aerobic exercise, too. In addition to helping you develop your balance, coordination, and fine motor skills, playing these games allows you to receive feedback in a method that is both risk-free and pleasant.

PHYSICAL ACTIVITIES

Socialization difficulties are more prevalent among teens with ADHD. They are frequently mistreated or misunderstood because of their actions. Despite the fact that they may be socially uncomfortable, they must develop the necessary discipline to cope with others.

Working together with other teenagers in cooperative sports like basketball, volleyball, and soccer has helped many teens with ADHD enhance their social skills. These sports offer little downtime, and you must be active on the court at all times.

You may get some exercise while playing a team sport and collaborating to win. These sports not only offer a chance for physical activity, but the abilities picked up may also be used to improve relationships with classmates.

Swimming lessons may be an ideal option if you are looking for a way to give yourself greater independence in a controlled, safe environment. ADHD teens have a great deal of surplus energy, which is expended by such activities. Due to the limited breathing while in the water, their bodies must work harder. Additionally, the motor skills, cognitive abilities, and physical fitness can all be enhanced by swimming.

CONCLUDING THE DISCUSSION

ADHD is an "invisible disability" that is frequently ignored by people unfamiliar with the illness. Socially unacceptable actions caused by ADHD symptoms are frequently attributed to other reasons. That is to say, these actions and the person who engages in them are frequently seen as impolite, selfish, careless, lazy, and ill-mannered.

Such stigmatizing terms eventually cause people with ADHD to be shunned by society. Many teens with ADHD experience emotional suffering due to social rejection, which can damage their lives by impairing their self-esteem throughout their lives.

Understanding ADHD in teens is a crucial first step in assisting them in coping with and managing their symptoms. With this understanding, parents, guardians, and educators may better support teens with ADHD by offering guidance, advice, and resources.

We took you on a ride to understand ADHD and its effects on teenagers. We guided you to manage your emotions, increase your self-esteem, discover your abilities, and build your confidence. We trust that you have gained knowledge from this experience and have the skills necessary to overcome any challenges standing in your way.

There were activities and other suggestions for you in this book that describe what you can do to improve in different aspects of your life. It shares guidance for you and your parents to follow and succeed in life. We urge you to continue looking ahead and pushing yourself to achieve your goals. Despite your ADHD, the sky is the limit for you!

You have the potential to achieve great things with perseverance and dedication. You must remember that you have complete control over your life and may steer it in whatever way you want.

Hopefully, you learned something here and found answers to your queries. Have a very blessed and managed life ahead!

Made in the USA
Monee, IL
25 June 2024